Bugs Are Beautiful!

A+ books®

Stunning Spiders

by Martha E. H. Rustad

Consultant:
Laura Jesse
Director, Plant and Insect Diagnostic Clinic
Iowa State University Extension
Ames, Iowa

• • •

CAPSTONE PRESS
a capstone imprint

T004477A

A+ Books are published by Capstone Press
1710 Roe Crest Drive, North Mankato, Minnesota 56003
www.mycapstone.com

Library of Congress Cataloging-in-Publication Data
Names: Rustad, Martha E. H. (Martha Elizabeth Hillman), 1975- author.
Title: Stunning spiders / by Martha E. H. Rustad.
Description: North Mankato, Minnesota : Capstone Press, [2017] | Series: Bugs are beautiful! | Series: A+ books | Audience: Ages 4-8. | Audience: K to grade 3. | Includes bibliographical references and index.
Identifiers: LCCN 2016032405 (print) | LCCN 2016041177 (ebook) | ISBN 9781515745006 (library binding) | ISBN 9781515745044 (pbk.) | ISBN 9781515745167 (eBook PDF)
Subjects: LCSH: Spiders–Juvenile literature.
Classification: LCC QL458.4 .R875 2017 (print) | LCC QL458.4 (ebook) | DDC 595.4/4–dc23
LC record available at https://lccn.loc.gov/2016032405

Editorial Credits
Editor, Abby Colich; Designer, Bobbie Nuytten; Media Researcher, Jo Miller; Production Specialist, Tori Abraham

Photo Credits
Alamy: Genevieve Valiee, 24; Minden Pictures: David Shale, 7; Newscom: Photoshop/NHPA/James Carmichael, 26; Rex Features via AP Images: Solent News/Jurgen Otto, 25; Shutterstock: aaltair, 19, Ajayptp, 30 (spiderlings), Arlo Hakola, 4 (legs), Boris Puhanic, 16, Bruce MacQueen, 10, Chuck Wagner, 29, CraigBurrows, 7, D. Kucharski K. Kucharska, 30 (adult), Dean Pennala, 6, Hajakely, 5 (top), Han maomin, 4 (web), Herman Wong HM, 28, Jansen Chua, 30 (eggs), kojihirano, 17, Linas T, 1, Linn Currie, 6, Linn Currie, 12, Linn Currie, 13, Marek Velechovsky, 27, Matteo photos, 22, Meister Photos, 8, Meister Photos, 9, Menno Schaefer, 21, nitat, 14, Pavel Krasensky, 18, popox, 5, (bottom), Puwadol Jaturawutthichai, map (throughout), RODINA OLENA, back cover (background), Sari ONeal, 15, Sebastian Janicki, cover, Vladimir Kim, 20, yauhenka, 11, zaidi razak, 30 (molt); SuperStock: BLANCHOT Philippe/Hemis.fr, 23

Note to Parents, Teachers, and Librarians

This Bugs Are Beautiful book uses full-color photographs and a nonfiction format to introduce the concept of spiders. Bugs Are Beautiful is designed to be read aloud to a pre-reader or to be read independently by an early reader. Photographs help listeners and early readers understand the text and concepts discussed. The book encourages further learning by including the following sections: Table of Contents, Glossary, Read More, Internet Sites, Critical Thinking Using the Common Core, and Index. Early readers may need assistance using these features.

Printed in the United States   4963

Table of Contents

Spiders Are **Stunning!**

web

eight legs

1 2 3 4 5 6 7 8

Wow! A bug scurries by your feet. Look at its bright colors! It has a cool pattern on its back. It has eight legs and lots of eyes. It's even hairy! This bug begins spinning a web. What is this creature? It's a spider!

Spiders don't have to be scary. They can be beautiful. Some are truly stunning!

eyes

Antilles **Pinktoe Tarantula**

pink "toe"

RANGE: Central America

SIZE: 6 inches (15 centimeters)

STUNNING FEATURE: Pink tip on legs

It's a rainbow of a spider! The Antilles pinktoe tarantula is blue as a spiderling. As it grows, it molts. The spider changes color with each molt. By adulthood its head is green. Its body is dark red. Its legs are black and purple. Can you guess what color the tip of its legs are? Pink! Even young spiders have pink "toes."

Black and Yellow Garden Spider

RANGE: North and Central America

SIZE: 1.1 inches (2.8 cm)

STUNNING SKILL: Spins zigzag in webs

Look at that zigzag! The black and yellow garden spider finds a sunny spot. It weaves a web. What does it do at night? It eats the web! Then it weaves a new one. A huge zigzag runs down its web.

Boing! If the spider feels unsafe, it bounces on the web. The moving web confuses predators.

Goldenrod Spider

RANGE: North America and Europe

SIZE: 0.4 inches (1 cm)

STUNNING SKILL: Changes color

Did that spider disappear? A goldenrod spider crawls onto a flower. Its body slowly changes color. Now the spider blends in with the flower petals. A bug visits the flower. It doesn't see the camouflaged spider. Eek! The spider makes a sneak attack. Its long front legs grab the bug. It's dinner time!

Can you see the spider?

Gooty **Tarantula**

Check out this blue spider!
The Gooty tarantula is born
brown. It changes color with
each molt. A young spider
turns lavender. It is blue by the
time it is fully grown. A flashy
white pattern runs down its
back. Yellow and white mark
its legs.

RANGE: India

SIZE: 7.9 inches (20 cm)

STUNNING COLOR: Bright blue

Green Lynx Spider

RANGE: North America

SIZE: 0.6 inches (1.6 cm)

STUNNING SKILL: Hunting

The green lynx spider does not spin a web. It hides and waits. Then it leaps onto its prey. Whoosh! It catches a bug.

This bright green spider blends in with leaves. A pattern runs down its back. Its legs are speckled with dots. Long hairs stick out of its legs.

Joro Spider

RANGE: China, Japan, North and South Korea, Taiwan

LEG SPAN: 3.9 inches (10 cm)

STUNNING SKILL: Weaves large webs

Look at that huge, shiny web! A Joro spider's web can reach 3.3 feet (1 meter) wide. Sunlight makes the webs look gold or yellow. The web catches lots of bugs for the spider to eat. Watch out! Even birds can get trapped in the large web.

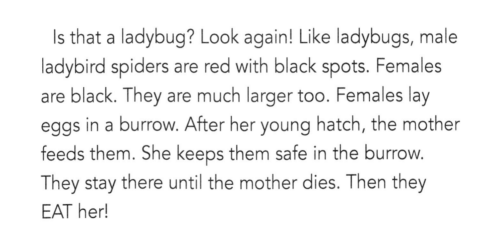

Ladybird Spider

Is that a ladybug? Look again! Like ladybugs, male ladybird spiders are red with black spots. Females are black. They are much larger too. Females lay eggs in a burrow. After her young hatch, the mother feeds them. She keeps them safe in the burrow. They stay there until the mother dies. Then they EAT her!

RANGE: Europe

SIZE: 0.6 inches (1.6 cm)

STUNNING FACT: Young eat their own mother

Marbled **Orb Weaver**

RANGE: United States, Canada, Europe

SIZE: 0.8 inches (2 cm)

STUNNING FEATURE: Pattern on body

Whoa! Check out the pattern on this spider! A marbled orb weaver's body is round like a tiny ball. Often the body is yellow. Sometimes it is white or orange. The legs are striped with orange, black, and white. Even its eggs are orange!

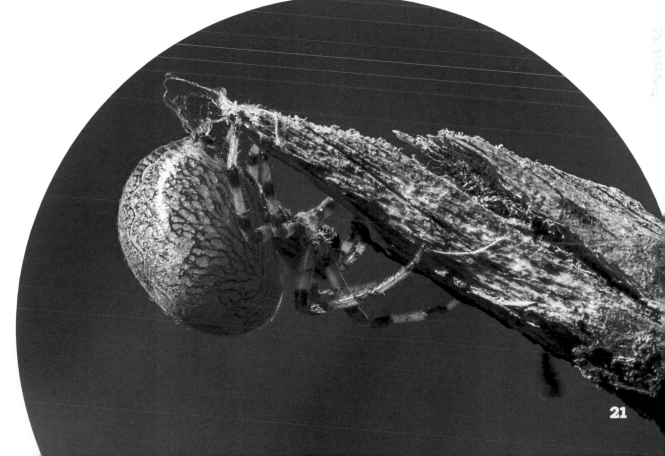

Mediterranean **Black Widow**

RANGE: Europe

SIZE: 0.6 inches (1.6 cm)

STUNNING FEATURE: Red spots

Look out! The Mediterranean black widow has spots of red. The red tells others that this spider is dangerous.

The spider catches prey in a sticky web. It also lays lines of silk on the ground. The silk traps bugs. Now the spider has even more food!

Peacock Spiders

RANGE: Australia

SIZE: 0.2 inches (0.5 cm)

STUNNING SKILL: Dances to show off colors

A male peacock spider likes to show off! He lifts his back and shakes it. Now his bright colors are on display. Then he lifts one or two legs. He wiggles them back and forth. He walks from side to side in a dance. Soon a female finds him.

Regal **Jumping Spider**

string of silk

Whee! A regal jumping spider soars into the air. It lands on a bug. The spider grabs its prey with two shiny pincers. It eats its meal.

When the spider jumps, it lets out a string of silk. If the spider misses its prey, the silk softens its fall.

pincers

RANGE: United States, Mexico, Caribbean

SIZE: 0.9 inches (2.2 cm)

STUNNING SKILL: Jump attack

RANGE: United States, Caribbean

SIZE: 0.5 inches (1.3 cm)

STUNNING FEATURE: Females have spikes

Beware! The female spiny orb weaver has spikes. The spikes scare away predators. Males have tiny bumps instead of spikes. The spiny orb weaver's body is white or yellow. It's covered in spots or stripes.

Life Cycle of a Spider

eggs

1 Spiders begin life as eggs.

2 Spiderlings hatch from the eggs.

3 As it grows, a spider molts.

shed outer layer

4 adult spider

Glossary

burrow (BUHR-oh)—an underground home of an animal

camouflage (KA-muh-flahj)—to blend in with one's surroundings

feature (FEE-chur)—an important part or quality of something

molt (MOLT)—to shed the hard outer covering while growing

pincer (PIN-sur)—a claw used to grasp

predator (PRED-uh-tur)—an animal that hunts another animal for food

prey (PRAY)—an animal hunted by another animal for food

range (RAYNJ)—an area where an animal mostly lives

spiderling (SPYE-dur-ling)—a young spider

venom (VEN-uhm)—a poisonous liquid made by some animals to stun or kill prey

Read More

Barton, Bethany. *I'm Trying to Love Spiders: (It Isn't Easy)*. New York: Viking, 2015.

Marsico, Katie. *Spiders Weave Webs*. Tell Me Why? Ann Arbor, Mich.: Cherry Lake Publishing, 2016.

Murray, Laura K. *Spiders*. Mankato, Minn.: Creative Education, 2016.

Internet Sites

FactHound offers a safe, fun way to find Internet sites related to this book. All of the sites on FactHound have been researched by our staff.

Here's all you do:

Visit *www.facthound.com*

Type in this code: 9781515745006

 Check out projects, games and lots more at
www.capstonekids.com

Critical Thinking Using the Common Core

1. How many legs do spiders have? (Key Idea and Details)

2. Page 27 says the spider has pincers. Use the glossary on page 31 to define pincer. (Craft and Structure)

3. Choose two spiders from the book. How are they alike? How are they different? (Integration of Knowledge and Ideas)

Index